VOT FOR ME!

Written by Abbie Rushton

Illustrated by María Díaz Perera

Collins

Dear parents and guardians,

I'm delighted to announce that applications for the student school council are open!

The school council is made up of one child from each class. The council meets weekly with the headteacher to discuss how the school should be run. A meeting might include topics such as:

• repairing or replacing playground equipment

• how to raise money for the school

• how the school can be more environmentally friendly.

To apply, your child must write a letter to their classmates explaining why they would make a good school councillor. Everyone who applies will also need to give a speech in assembly. Then children will vote to decide who will make the best school councillors.

I look forward to seeing your children's applications by Friday!

With best wishes,

Ms Chatterjee

Ms Chatterjee
Headteacher

1 MONDAY: THE LETTER

"This sounds great!" Albie's mum said, showing Albie the crumpled letter she'd pulled from the bottom of his bag. "Are you going to apply to be on the school council?"

Albie blushed. "I'm not sure," he mumbled.

"What was that idea you mentioned last week? You wanted to make a wildflower area in the corner of the school field to attract bees. That's a great plan!"

Albie shrugged and stared at the floor. It felt like it wasn't just Mum looking at him, but everyone in the whole school!

"Well, if you were on the school council, you could maybe make it happen."

"I suppose so," Albie replied, putting his coat on as he headed towards the back door.

Mum sighed softly and followed Albie outside.

Albie knelt by their tomato plants, checking them for slugs.

Mum sat down beside him. She breathed deeply. "I love the smell of tomatoes," she said.

"Me too," Albie replied, rubbing a leaf between his fingers.

"We are a funny pair of tomato-sniffers!" Mum giggled.

They sat in silence for a few minutes, listening to the murmur of the wind in the grass and a bird chirping in next door's garden.

Oscar the cat padded over to them.

"Do you think Oscar ever gets butterflies in his tummy?" Albie asked Mum.

"Maybe," Mum replied. "If he decides to eat some butterflies!" She nudged Albie and they laughed.

"There you both are!" a voice boomed across the garden. "Hi, big man!"

"Hi, Tanaka," Albie said as he and Mum jumped up to greet Albie's stepdad.

Albie gave him a high-five. Tanaka pretended to stumble backwards. "Whoah! Did you get stronger overnight?"

Albie chuckled. "Do you want to play football?" he asked as Oscar rubbed against Tanaka's legs to say hello.

Tanaka loosened his tie. "Do I? Let me just change out of these boring work clothes first. I need to run if I'm going to score any goals against you."

Albie jogged down the garden to grab the football.

It wasn't long before he was lost in the game with Tanaka, and all thoughts of the school council had vanished.

Dear **Albie**,

I know exactly what you, the voters, care about.
I know that you LOVE Fishy Friday. If I were voted in,
I would make sure that Fishy Friday happened EVERY
DAY OF THE WEEK! That's right – you could eat fish
fingers until they came out of your ears!

Also, you know when your mum says stuff like: "I don't
know where your odd socks disappear to!" Well, this
wouldn't be a problem if I was voted in, because every
Wednesday would be officially 'odd sock day'. Even the
teachers would have to join in!

Finally, I plan to introduce a 'tea tax' on teachers.
Every time they drink a cup of tea (or coffee) – and
you know that's a lot – they'd have to give us all
a biscuit. And not a rubbish biscuit, either. It would
have to be a chocolate one.

Go Team Zainab!

From,

Zainab

2 TUESDAY: SHAKE THINGS UP

"Hi, Albie!" said Zainab, waving cheerfully as Albie hung his coat up at school.

"Er … hi!" Albie replied. Zainab didn't usually chat to him much.

"Did you get my letter in your tray?"

"Yes, thanks."

"Great. So can I count on your vote?"

"I'm not sure. I haven't had any other letters yet. I was thinking –"

"Don't agree to anything, Albie!" someone interrupted.

It was Jai, Albie's best friend. "I'm going to apply as well. I hear you get a free badge if you get on the school council."

"Well, you can kiss that badge goodbye, Jai!" Zainab replied. "A promise of free biscuits and unlimited fish fingers? I think I've already won."

"Unless they're chocolate biscuits, I don't think anyone's going to take you seriously," Jai said.

Zainab smiled smugly. "You clearly haven't read my letter yet! Like I said, Jai, I've already won. See you, Albie," she said as she walked off.

"Are you going to apply, Albie?" Jai asked.

Albie shook his head. "Don't think so."

Jai looked surprised. "But the free badge!
Plus, I heard you get time out of lessons
to go to the school council meetings.
I really hope it's time out of
maths lessons."

"You're good at maths," Albie pointed out.

Jai did an exaggerated yawn. "Yeah, but
it's boring! Hey, want to hang out
at breaktime?"

"Sure!"

Jai grinned. "I've got a new idea for a dance.
Mum let me stay up to watch Dazzling Dancers
on Saturday and I want to show you my routine."

Jai started to spin around the classroom.

"That's quite enough, thank you, Jai,"
said their teacher, Mrs Chen, appearing
out of nowhere. "We don't dance in
the classroom."

At breaktime, Mrs Chen stopped Albie before he went outside. "I heard you talking about the school council elections earlier," she said.

Albie raised his eyebrows. Teachers really do see and hear everything!

"Are you going to apply?" Mrs Chen asked.

A ripple of fear spread across Albie's stomach.

"I don't think so," Albie replied. "I won't have a very good chance."

"You have some great ideas, Albie," Mrs Chen pointed out.

Another ripple.

Mrs Chen continued. "You mentioned having a box in school where people can bring in old school uniforms to either donate or swap. You could make a big difference."

The ripples turned to waves.

Albie edged closer to the door.

"OK, I'll think about it," he said, before rushing out to find Jai.

Dear **Albie**,

Vote for Jai!

Do you think things look a bit boring around here? Fed up with the same old blue and grey uniforms? If you'd like to SHAKE THINGS UP and make everything a bit more FUN, you need to elect me!

If I'm on the school council, I promise to change our dull school uniforms into sequinned trousers. I bet it'll cheer up the teachers to see loads of sparkly colours in our classrooms, instead of a sea of grey. It's a win for EVERYONE!

I also plan on upgrading the school logo. Don't get me wrong ... I like trees. Trees are important, but they're not exciting. Imagine if the school logo was a luminous dolphin instead. Now that would really stand out!

From,

Jai

PS: I would also replace maths lessons with ballet and tap dance lessons.

3 WEDNESDAY: A SNEAKY CAMPAIGN

"There's no way I'm wearing anything with sequins!" Zainab announced to Eden at breaktime.

"Yeah, but just imagine – no more maths lessons EVER!" Eden said.

Zainab snorted, "Jai can't stop maths lessons. No one has that power."

"What did you think, Albie?" Jai asked.

Albie smiled at the hopeful look on Jai's face. He wasn't always as confident as he appeared.

"I liked your dolphin logo," Albie said, although privately he thought it might be a bit confusing for a school called 'Cherry Tree' ...

"I'm going to run for school council!" Eden said suddenly.

"Why?" Zainab asked.

Eden shrugged. "Dunno. I just think the badges look cool."

At lunchtime, Jai and Albie ended up at the back of the queue in the canteen. "It takes so looooong!" Jai moaned, clutching his stomach dramatically. "I'm so hungry."

"I had this idea that we should all go to lunch at slightly different times," Albie said. "If Class 1 went first, then Class 2 five minutes later, and so on, it would mean we don't all have to queue."

Jai frowned. "Class 6 wouldn't have much play time."

"No, they'd still have an hour," Albie explained. "Lunchtimes would end at different times, too."

"That's a good idea!" said Jai. "You should tell Mrs Chen."

"I did. She thinks I should be on the school council."

"That's an even better idea!" exclaimed Jai. "Why didn't I think of that?"

"Because then you'd have some competition!" Albie laughed.

After lunch, Jai and Albie rushed outside. Albie headed straight to the top corner of the playing field. It would be a perfect spot for a little wildflower patch – right in the sun.

"Check out this cartwheel, Albie!" Jai shouted.
Albie turned around to look, just as a football thudded into Jai's back.

Jai fell to the ground.

One of the older boys ran up. "Sorry. Are you OK?"

Jai nodded, but Albie saw his bottom lip wobble slightly.

The older boy ran back to his football match and Albie helped Jai up.

"Thanks, Albie," Jai said. "You know what? You *should* apply for the school council. You have good ideas, and you're a good friend. You like to help people."

Albie just smiled in response. Everyone was telling him to give it a go. What if he did?

TOP SECRET

Dear **Albie**,

Do not show this letter to ANYONE else. In fact, you should tear it into little pieces after you've read it. But don't flush it down the toilet - that would block it.

I am launching a secret campaign against Zainab and Jai. Who wants tap dance lessons and stinky fish fingers? NONE of us!

Who wants free crisps? ALL of us!

So that's my promise. Vote for me and I'll give you some crisps out of my lunchbox. They will either be ready salted or salt and vinegar. No special requests - I don't 'do' smelly crisps. So, no cheese and onion, prawn cocktail or anything like that.

Take it or leave it.

Eden

4 THURSDAY: A SECRET FOR SUCCESS

"Eden!" Zainab shouted as she walked into school with Albie and Jai. "Free crisps? That was a sneaky idea."

"Can I just check?" Jai asked. "Is it one bag of crisps per person, or one for all your voters?"

Eden shrugged, looking as deflated as an empty packet of crisps.

Albie wasn't sure that the number of bags of crisps made a huge difference. Eden wasn't promising anything that would actually help the school.

Albie wondered if she'd really applied because of the badge, or if she was trying to impress her mum. Eden's sister was Head Girl.

"I'm not sharing!" Zainab declared. "I will vote for you, though."

"You're not allowed to vote if you're applying to be a school councillor," Albie pointed out.

Zainab looked disappointed. "Oh, I was looking forward to some crisps. My grandad always puts rice cakes in my packed lunch. They taste like cardboard."

After school, Tanaka and Albie baked some cupcakes for Mum.

"So, what's all this about the school council, then?" Tanaka asked as Albie weighed out the flour.

Albie explained that people had sent out letters and that they would be voting tomorrow.

"Who are you going to vote for?" Tanaka said, cracking an egg with one hand.

Albie shrugged. "None of their ideas are that great, to be honest."

"Why don't you apply, then? I bet you've got some great ideas."

"I do. I just ... don't want to speak in front of everyone. We have to give a speech in assembly."

Tanaka turned on the food processor. Albie watched the mixture. That's how his head would feel if he gave a speech – everything churning around and mixed up.

Tanaka started to mouth random words at Albie, pretending to talk. Albie giggled. "I know you're not saying anything!" he shouted.

When Tanaka turned the food processor off, he said, "I have to give speeches for work sometimes. I don't much like it, either. Want to know my secret?"

Albie raised an eyebrow as he dolloped a spoon of cake mix in a cupcake case. "Do you imagine everyone dressed as clowns?"

"No. That would just make me laugh! I take a few deep breaths, then I imagine myself delivering the speech calmly and confidently, and I picture it going really well."

Albie thought for a minute. "I don't have much time now, though. The applications have to be in tomorrow."

"Well, what are we waiting for, then? Let's get these cupcakes in the oven and work out what you're going to say!"

SWAP SHOP

LUNCHTIME

WILDFLOWER PATCH

Dear **Jai**,

I think you should vote for me. I'd like to be a school councillor because I have some good ideas for how to make the school better.

My first idea is to make a wildflower patch in the top corner of the playing field. This would be good for the bees as it would give them food and shelter.

My next idea is to have a 'swap shop' for school uniforms. It could just be a box in school where parents can drop off old school uniforms that we've grown out of and maybe pick up new ones.

Finally, I think we should change lunchtimes so each class goes in at a different time, starting with Class 1. They'd only be 5 minutes apart, but it would help with the queuing times.

Thank you for reading this,

Albie

5 Friday: Fighting the storm

"Albie!" Jai cried, running up to Albie and waving the letter. "You did it!"

Albie nodded nervously. His stomach was a stormy sea, sloshing around.

"It's great!" Jai said.

"Well done, Albie," Eden added.

"No chocolate biscuits for you, then," Zainab said. "Only joking! Good job."

Albie grinned at his friends and the storm calmed a little.

Mrs Chen started the lesson, though Albie's brain was full of questions, like bees buzzing around. What if he forgot what he was going to say? What if they all laughed at him?

Albie remembered what Tanaka had said, then he visualised himself speaking clearly and confidently, and everyone clapping at the end.

"Right, time to line up for assembly,"
Mrs Chen announced.

Albie felt a wave of panic. He took several
deep breaths. It felt like they were blowing
the storm clouds away.

On the way to assembly, Mrs Chen whispered,
"Whatever happens, Albie, I'm really proud of you."

Albie smiled.

"Hello, everyone," Ms Chatterjee said. "I've enjoyed reading your wonderful applications for school council this week. In a moment we're going to hear from the people who have applied."

Albie gulped. Next to him, Jai was jiggling his legs excitedly, or was it nervously? Albie wondered if Jai could hear his heart beating. It was like great big bangs of thunder!

Ms Chatterjee continued, "When they've finished speaking, you'll each get a piece of paper and you need to tick one person from each class you'd like to vote for. Mrs Chen will count up the votes and we'll announce the winners at the end of assembly."

Albie watched as Zainab, Jai and Eden each stood up to speak. They seemed so confident. How did they do it? He closed his eyes and imagined himself being confident.

"Well done, Eden," Ms Chatterjee said as everyone clapped. "And next we have … Albie!"

Albie stood on shaking legs and made his way to the front. Hundreds of pairs of eyes stared back at him, waiting for him to speak …

"Erm ... hello everyone. I'm Albie. Hope you all got my letter. I ... er ... Sorry it was a bit late.

Anyway, I ... well, I think I would be a good councillor. I can't promise you odd socks, sequins or free crisps. I just think I'd be good because – like I said in the letter – I have some great ideas for how to make our school better. And I like to help people. I'd like to help all of you if I was voted into the school council.

So, that's it, really. Thanks!"

Albie blushed as everyone clapped, then he sat back down as quickly as possible.

The rest of the assembly seemed to take forever. Finally, Mrs Chen came back in with a piece of paper. Albie held his breath. The results!

Ms Chatterjee grinned, then began to read from the paper. She started with Class 1. Albie held his breath until she said, "The school councillor for Class 3 is ... Albie Cooper."

Did Albie imagine that? He froze.

Then Jai whispered, "Albie! You did it!"

Albie felt a rush of pride. She *did* say his name! Albie couldn't believe it. He'd done it.

For a moment, he couldn't move.

He heard Zainab sigh loudly behind him and mutter, "They chose bees over biscuits? Unbelievable!"

Then Jai tapped Albie on the shoulder. "Get up! You have to go to the front."

Albie scrambled to his feet and walked to the front in a daze as everyone clapped. It was just how he'd pictured it. He'd really won!

6 THREE MONTHS LATER

Mum, Tanaka and Albie admired the school wildflower patch. The air was full of the happy hum of bees and the melody of children playing on the field before they went home.

"We're proud of you, big man," Tanaka said.

Mum ruffled his hair. Albie beamed. A glow of pride spread over him, like stepping into a hot bath.

Jai ran up in his favourite sequinned top. "Hey Albie! 'Sparkle day' is great! I hope we've raised loads of money for the new compost bin."

Zainab headed over. She pulled up her trousers and grinned. "Odd socks! Told you I wouldn't wear sparkles. I still donated some money, though."

As Eden walked past, she threw a packet of salt and vinegar crips at Zainab. "Here you go, Zainab! A gift from me."

"See you later, guys!" Albie called.

Albie took one last look at his wildflower patch. A butterfly took off, then soared high in the sky. *That's where butterflies belong,* Albie thought. *In the sky, not in tummies.*

Then he followed Mum and Tanaka to the car, his school council badge glinting proudly in the sun.

Worried about doing something that makes you feel nervous? You can do it!

1 Take some deep breaths if your tummy is churning.

2 Picture yourself doing an amazing job.

3 Listen to advice from others.

4 Don't let your fears stop you from flying.

By Albie Cooper,
School Councillor

✿ Ideas for reading ✿

Written by Gill Matthews
Primary Literacy Consultant

Reading objectives:
- make inferences on the basis of what is being said and done
- answer and ask questions
- predict what might happen on the basis of what has been read so far

Spoken language objectives:
- articulate and justify answers, arguments and opinions
- participate in discussions, presentations, performances, role play, improvisations and debates

Curriculum links: Relationships education: Caring friendships

Word count: 3099

Interest words: blushed, mumbled, shrugged

Resources: paper and pencils

Build a context for reading
- Ask children to look at the front cover and to read the title.
- Discuss what "vote" means and whether children have ever taken part in a vote.
- Read the back cover blurb and ask children what they think is going to happen in the story. If necessary, explain the concept of a school council.

Understand and apply reading strategies
- Read pp2–3 aloud. Ask children what they think would make a good school councillor.
- Read pp4–11 aloud, using meaning, punctuation and dialogue to help you read with appropriate expression.
- Discuss children's impressions of Albie.
- Ask what they think of Zainab's letter and whether she would make a good school councillor.